POEMS ABOUT

LOVE

By

Suru Ayo

ISBN: 978-969-2992-90-9

Table Of Contents

Foreword

When I was younger, I used to believe that love was something that happened to somebody else. I thought that we only found it in stories and movies. As I grew older, I realized that love is something that we create for ourselves. It's something that we search for and yearn for. It's the heartwarming feeling that tells us that we're not alone in this world. It's the light in the darkness and the hope that keeps us going. It's the love that we share with our families, friends, and lovers. It's the love that makes the world feel right.

1

You light up my life like lightning

You make everything feel okay

And I know that I could never survive

WITHOUT YOU!.

2

I wonder why we love

Some things are hard to understand

But when we find someone we care for

We know what it is that we have

And we'll never let them go

We love because it's something we should

It's something we always want to experience

And when we're with that special someone

We feel complete and happy inside.

3

Love is a mystery

Love is a magic

Love is an enchantment

A love that binds us together

For eternity

A love so strong and so powerful

A love so pure and so beautiful

A love that will never end.

4

Love is the colour of the sky

And the sound of the waves

The tingle of a kiss

And the warmth of a hug

Love is the way that the world turns

And the happiness that we feel

It's the light in our eyes

And the joy in our hearts.

5

Love is patient and kind

It knows no boundaries

It doesn't mind if you're weak or strong

Love is always there

It will never leave you

Love is the answer

To all our prayers.

6

Love is a burning flame

That never dies,

And it's always burning

In our hearts.

It's the most beautiful

thing in the world

And we couldn't survive

Without it.

7

⌘

Love is in the air,

we can't deny it,

It's one of the most precious things,

We just can't help but feel it.

The way we look at one another,

It just melts our hearts,

And we can't imagine

living without it.

We know that love is worth fighting for,

And no matter what happens,

We will always remember

the love we Shared together.

8

How sweet it is to be loved

To feel somebody's arms surround you

pledging their love to you

For being who you are

To know that you're someone's world

And that they will never want to be without you

Is something incomparable

And nothing can ever take that away

The feeling of being loved

Is something that is truly divine

It fills us with warmth

And makes us feel complete.

9

Love is a light in the darkness

It guides us and protects us

Love is a song that never ends

It brings happiness and peace

Love is the only thing that truly matters

And it always will.

10

Love is a song that never dies

It's a flame that burns with burning heat

Even in the darkest of nights

Love never dies, never fades away.

11

When I think of you

I feel so happy

I can't wait to spend my life with you

I love you so much

I can't imagine my life without you

You are the most special person in the world to me

Whenever I am with you

I feel like nothing can bring me down

I love how you are always there for me

And how you make me feel so loved

I can't wait to.

12

Love is like a sweet spring breeze

A warmth that fills the air with ease

A passion that will never cease

A feeling of joy and peace

Love is like a melody divine

Rising from the depths of time

A gentle current that binds

The heart of yours and mine

Love is like a whisper of understanding

It carries us through life's demanding

It calms us in times of social unrest

It brings us hope and makes us blessed

Love is like a sunset so grand

Colors of orange, red and sand

A portrait that paints the sky

A sign of our forever tie.

13

Roses are red, violets are blue,

Love can be sweet, and sometimes cruel too.

It can bring joy, tears, or heartache,

We all need it, no matter our age.

Love can be kind, passionate, or deep,

It can break hearts, and keep us from sleep.

Relentless and free, it's a powerful thing,

Enduring at times, loving beyond anything.

Love is the centre of life,

It's more than companionship, husband, and wife.

It's joys, it's sorrows, it's secrets, and surprises,

Love completes us, it puts us at ease.

It can make us kind, it can make us brave,

And when shared in life, it truly can save.

So when together, and sometimes apart,

Love will continue, to heal the broken heart.

14

Love passes through like a gentle breeze,

Softly touching hearts with ease.

A beauty existing beneath the stars,

A precious bond that can travel far.

A love that is warm and so inviting,

Restoring the soul yet always exciting.

A connection unlike any other,

Life without it can feel so much colder.

The heart whispers and feelings arise,

Ending the sadness and filling our skies.

A depth of emotion without compare,

Flowing through veins with love that is rare.

It bolsters and strengthens one's might,

A tenderness feeling that truly can brighten night.

A passion powerful and so wise,

That can carry us with love through all of our lives.

15

Love can be delicate, like a soft twinkling melody

Or it can be bold, like crackling thunder in the night

It can be playful, like a whisper tickling your ear

Or it can be firm, like a myriad stars shining in the sky

Love is a brilliant thing that is never ending

It has no preferred form, and never sets a limit

It's always ready to forgive, even when it may seem
undeserving

It's a special bond that can never be broken

From the joy of companionship to the comfort of a hug

Love comes in many shapes, even when times get rough

It can make us feel alive, renewed and reborn

Love is a bond that can never be torn.

16

Love is a golden star

That glistens in the sky

It twinkles above us

As we look up so high

Love is a summer breeze

That cools the warmest days

It blows away our sadness

And shows us brighter ways

Love is a healing salve

For all our broken dreams

It wraps us in its arms

And brightens what it means

Love is a special gift

Sent down from above

It helps us to survive

With bumps and and bends of love.

17

The warmth radiates through me,

From the moment that I hear your name,

My heart flutters, my cheeks pinken,

At the thought of your everlasting flame.

Every time I see you,

I can't help but to fall a bit more in love,

My heart leaps, my spirit soars,

Whenever our paths do cross.

My love for you transcends the groggy depths,

Of so many of my sleepy nights,

And for the times I must be apart,

Your memory is my sweet reprieve.

I am grateful for all the mornings,

That I get to spend in your wonderous light,

For it is your love that keeps me safe,

From the muck and mire of my sorrows plight.

Your strength persistent and brilliant,

Your soul so gentle and true,

It is love that's been blessed to us,

In this life me and you.

18

Love is a feeling like none other

It comes and it leaves like the changing weather

But when it sticks around memories are made

That last through all the time and space

Love crafts stories of heartache and joy

Like a rollercoaster it can make us enjoy

A love that never changes through the change of time

It's a special bond that grows like a vine

A love that brightens a dark dismal day

A love that's felt both near and far away

A special bond that's incomparable

And nothing else will be as memorable

This love humans need like the air that we breathe

And it's a beautiful feeling that will never leave

A love so strong, it can make us soar

Filling our souls with nothing but love evermore.

19

Love leaves its mark

A passionate spark

It catches us off guard

And leaves us enthraled

It can be a constant reminder

We can't help but surrender

To the feeling deep down inside

A warmth that can never hide

It may come at the most unexpected times

And if it lingers too long it can cross lines

It can fill us with joy and hope

Or throw us completely off the cope

Love is a powerful thing, it's a beauty to behold

It can heal the broken heart and make us feel whole

Sometimes it lasts forever and sometimes it just ends

But it will always be remembered, no matter how
long it's been.

20

Love is patient and kind

It doesn't seek its own

It is not easily angered nor will it ever be

It rejoices in the truth and puts up with all kinds

Love never fails

It never wavers and never fades away

It is always present and never takes away

Its joys will brighten each and every day

It gives strength in times of weakness and makes us braver

Love shall conquer all and forever remain

Its bond will bind us and heal our pain

It will fill us with warmth and bestow us kind-heartedness

No matter what others may try, love will prevail!.

21

Love is an emotion so deep and so true,

It carries us when there's nothing left to do.

The emotion of happiness and the joy inside,

It can make us feel alive or bring us to collide.

Love is strong, sometimes it can leave you breathless,

It can send you to heights of ecstasy or deep dark distress.

It doesn't matter who you are, if you don't feel love, you're lost,

You must accept it in order to stay on the right path.

Love can bring us pain and anguish at times,

But it can also be filled with a warmth that shines.

It can be terrifying, powerful, or awaken us from our sleep,

It makes us realize there's something special out there just for me.

Love may be painful, but it's a chance we all must take,

For without it we may never truly awake.

So open up your hearts and share love with everyone,

It's the only way to make our world a brighter sun.

22

❦

Love is a sense like no other

Joyful and mellow, it will not smother

Rides like a wave that comes with ease

It warms the heart and brings peace

Love is like a bright light in the night

A blanket over wrongs and right

It's a symbol of care, that holds strong

It can mend matters of which we were long

People have searched for feelings like this

Love can last and never miss

It will never die, no matter the cost

For it gives something that nothing has lost.

23

Love can be so unexplainable

It's a sweet tale not too traditional

It's a powerful feeling so strong

It can last all day long

It shows us joy, and brings us peace

It can heal our hurt and grief

Love can also be like a current

It can bring excitement, yet be divergent

It binds two persons together tight

Making sure to stay in each others sight

Though it can come it can also leave

A pain that can never be relieved

It's a feeling that's so good to have

But it can hurt you so bad

This beautiful emotion that shows us true care

Will remain forever, through thick and thin air.

Made in the USA
Monee, IL
07 July 2026